First Facts®

Who Lived Here?

DESERT
Communities
PAST and PRESENT

by Cindy Jenson-Elliott

Consultant:
Zoe Burkholder, PhD
Assistant Professor, College of Education
and Human Services
Montclair State University
Montclair, New Jersey

CAPSTONE PRESS
a capstone imprint

P9-CLX-767

First Facts are published by Capstone Press,
1710 Roe Crest Drive, North Mankato, Minnesota 56003
www.capstonepub.com

Library of Congress Cataloging-in-Publication Data
Jenson-Elliott, Cindy.
Desert communities past and present / by Cindy Jenson-Elliott.
     pages cm. – (First facts. Who lived here?)
Includes bibliographical references and index.
Summary: "Compares and contrasts the way people lived in a
North American desert over the course of centuries"— Provided by
publisher.
  ISBN 978-1-4765-4059-7 (library binding)
  ISBN 978-1-4765-5141-8 (paperback)
  ISBN 978-1-4765-5994-0 (eBook PDF)
1. Human settlements—United States—History—Juvenile literature.
2. Deserts—United States—Juvenile literature. 3. Desert people—
United States—Juvenile literature. I. Title.
  HN57.J46 2014
  306.0915'4—dc23   2013036079

Editorial Credits
Brenda Haugen, editor; Juliette Peters, designer; Svetlana Zhurkin,
media researcher; Charmaine Whitman, production specialist

Photo Credits
Alamy: North Wind Picture Archives, 13; Bridgeman Art Library:
Private Collection/Francisco Vasquez de Coronado Making His Way
across New Mexico, Frederic Remington, 11; Corbis: Horace Bristol, 17,
National Geographic Society/Frederick I. Monsen, 15; Getty Images:
National Geographic, 7; Newscom: Danita Delimont Photography/
Julien McRoberts, cover (left); Shutterstock: Ami Parikh, 5, Anton
Foltin, 20, Brocreative, 19, Doug Meek, 9, Naaman Abreu, cover
(hogan), Samiah Samin (background), cover and throughout,
Sourav and Joyeeta, cover (middle back), 1, 2, 23, 24

Printed in the United States of America in North Mankato, Minnesota.
092013   007771CGS14

TABLE OF CONTENTS

PEOPLE COME TO THE DESERT 4

HUNTING AND GATHERING 6

CLIFF DWELLERS 8

SPANIARDS ARRIVE 10

RANCHING 12

ROADS CROSS THE DESERT 14

TOWNS SPRING UP 16

DESERT CITIES BLOOM 18

CLEAN ENERGY 20

AMAZING BUT TRUE! 21

Glossary 22

Read More 23

Internet Sites 23

Critical Thinking Using
   the Common Core 24

Index 24

PEOPLE COME to the DESERT
10,000 BC to 300 BC

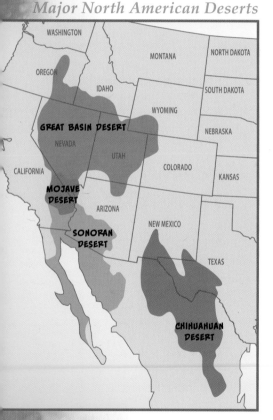

Major North American Deserts

People came to the North American deserts thousands of years ago. Some came from the northwest and what is now Siberia. Others came from the south from what is now Mexico.

The people used stone tools and moved as the seasons changed to find food. Men hunted animals with sticks and spears. Women gathered plants. They always lived near water.

FACT
Desert people sometimes drew pictures on rocks that showed how they lived.

EXTREME WEATHER

Deserts are hot in the summer and cold in the winter. But all year they are very dry. Deserts get less than 10 inches (25.4 centimeters) of rain each year. Desert plants and animals can live with little water.

HUNTING AND GATHERING
⬤— AD 250 —⬤

People lived in caves near **oases** and rivers. The water allowed trees, grass, and other plants to grow. The people wove grass into baskets. They hunted animals and gathered seeds, leaves, and roots.

Flooding made the soil near rivers **rich**. People began planting seeds and farming.

---

oasis—a place in a desert where there is water for plants, animals, and people

rich—having many nutrients to help plants grow

Hunters aim at a deer with bows and arrows.

CLIFF DWELLERS

1200s

Large **communities** were built on **cliffs** in the 1200s. The cliff homes kept people safe from animals and from their enemies.

But the people still depended on the rivers. Women planted corn, beans, and squash. They dug **trenches** from the river to water their **crops**. If a river dried up, the people moved to another source of water.

community—a group of people who live in the same area

cliff—a high, steep rock face

trench—a long, deep area dug into the ground

crop—a plant farmers grow in large amounts, usually for food

People built homes high on cliffs to stay safe.

FACT

Men were the hunters in their communities. They hunted deer, rabbits, squirrels, and other animals with bows and arrows.

SPANIARDS ARRIVE

1500s

When Spanish explorers and settlers arrived in the 1500s, life changed for many desert people. Spaniards brought wheat, horses, and cattle to the desert. They used metal farm tools. They built **adobe** homes.

> **FACT**
>
> The Spanish also brought diseases that were new to the desert **natives**. Many desert people died from these new diseases.

adobe—bricks made from mud and straw, dried and hardened by the heat of the sun

natives—people who originally lived in a certain place

Spanish explorers bring horses to the desert.

RANCHING

1850s

As American settlers moved west, the lives of those living in deserts changed again. American ranchers brought horses and **herds** of cattle. The cattle trampled plants, and horses scared away game animals.

RAISING SHEEP

Ranchers did not just raise cattle. Some raised sheep. Desert natives also began to raise sheep for their wool. They wove wool into blankets. Sometimes they made pictures in the blankets that told stories.

A rancher moves his herd of cattle.

The new settlers also brought guns. The guns quickly replaced bows and arrows for hunting.

herd—a large group of animals that lives or moves together

ROADS CROSS THE DESERT

1900s

Wood-**plank** roads made travel easier in many parts of the desert. Horses and carts brought food and other goods. Trading posts were built to sell goods. Native people sold jewelry, blankets, and pottery.

The new roads also brought more people. Some wanted to relax in the **hot springs**. More farmers came to the desert too. **Irrigation** made more land available for farming.

Travelers cross the desert in a horse-drawn wagon.

plank—a piece of wood that holds something in place

hot spring—a mineral water source where the temperature is higher than that of its surroundings

irrigation—supplying water to crops using a system of pipes or trenches

TOWNS SPRING UP

LATE 1930s

New **paved** roads and a railroad brought goods to the desert. Trucks and railroad cars carried food and other products. They also brought wood, which was used to build houses and businesses.

Towns began to grow. Stores and **tourism** provided jobs in towns. Many people moved to these towns. They bought food instead of farming or hunting.

pave—to cover a road or other surface with a hard material such as asphalt

tourism—the business of taking care of visitors to a country or place

Towns such as Eureka, California, grew in the desert as roads improved.

DESERT CITIES BLOOM

● — 1970s — ●

Vacationers flocked to desert cities for fun in the sun. They came by car, train, bus, and airplane to visit the desert.

Wires carried electricity to desert cities from power plants far away. The electricity powered everything from lights to air conditioners. The air conditioners kept homes and businesses cool year round.

FACT

Spas were often located at hot springs. People enjoyed soaking in the warm water.

Vacationers come to the desert to golf and enjoy the outdoors.

POLLUTION BECOMES A PROBLEM

Airplanes, cars, and power plants can cause pollution. This pollution can harm the air, water, and soil. In the 1970s the desert air near cities was sometimes brown with pollution.

pollution—materials that hurt Earth's water, air, and land

CLEAN ENERGY
2000s

Many people living in the desert try to use **resources** wisely. Wind **turbines** spin as the wind blows. **Solar panels** grace thousands of rooftops. Each turbine and solar panel makes clean energy that does not cause pollution. People also try to save water. They put desert plants in their yards instead of grass.

resource—something useful or valuable to a place or person

turbine—device with curved blades connected to a central shaft that spins as wind passes over the blades

solar panel—a flat surface that collects sunlight and turns it into power

The deserts of southern California have more earthquakes than almost anywhere in the world. Sometimes there are more than 60 earthquakes a month in the same area!

The earthquakes are caused by two pieces of Earth's crust pushing together. When too much pressure builds up, the pieces slip past each other, and an earthquake rattles the ground. Many desert earthquakes occur on the San Andreas fault, a crack where two pieces of Earth's crust meet.

GLOSSARY

adobe (uh-DOH-bee)—bricks made from mud and straw, dried and hardened by the heat of the sun

cliff (KLIF)—a high, steep rock face

community (kuh-MYOO-nuh-tee)—a group of people who live in the same area

crop (KROP)—a plant farmers grow in large amounts, usually for food

herd (HURD)—a large group of animals that lives or moves together

hot spring (HAHT SPRING)—a mineral water source where the temperature is higher than that of its surroundings

irrigation (ihr-uh-GAY-shuhn)—supplying water to crops using a system of pipes or trenches

natives (NAY-tivz)—people who originally lived in a certain place

oasis (oh-AY-siss)—a place in a desert where there is water for plants, animals, and people

pave (PAYV)—to cover a road or other surface with a hard material such as asphalt

plank (PLANK)—a piece of wood that holds something in place

pollution (puh-LOO-shuhn)—materials that hurt Earth's water, air, and land

resource (REE-sorss)—something useful or valuable to a place or person

rich (RICH)—having many nutrients to help plants grow

solar panel (SOH-lur PAN-uhl)—a flat surface that collects sunlight and turns it into power

tourism (TOOR-i-zuhm)—the business of taking care of visitors to a country or place

trench (TRENCH)—a long, deep area dug into the ground

turbine (TUR-bine)—device with curved blades connected to a central shaft that spins as wind passes over the blades

READ MORE

Auch, Alison. *Life in the Desert.* Habitats Around the World. Mankato, Minn.: Capstone Press, 2012.

Callery, Sean. *Life Cycles: Desert.* Life Cycles. London: Kingfisher, 2012.

Waldron, Melanie. *Deserts.* Habitat Survival. Chicago: Raintree, 2013.

INTERNET SITES

FactHound offers a safe, fun way to find Internet sites related to this book. All of the sites on FactHound have been researched by our staff.

Here's all you do:

Visit *www.facthound.com*

Type in this code: 9781476540597

Super-cool stuff!

Check out projects, games and lots more at
www.capstonekids.com

CRITICAL THINKING USING THE COMMON CORE

1. Look at the Fact on page 10. What is the author trying to explain? (Craft and Structure)

2. How did electricity make life better in the desert? (Key Ideas and Details)

INDEX

cattle, 10, 12
caves, 6
cliffs, 8
communities, 8

diseases, 10

earthquakes, 21
electricity, 18, 20
explorers, 10

farming, 6, 8, 10, 14, 16

horses, 10, 12, 14
hot springs, 14, 18
hunting, 4, 6, 9, 13, 16

irrigation, 14

jobs, 16

Mexico, 4

oases, 6

plants, 4, 6, 12, 20
pollution, 18, 20

railroads, 16
ranchers, 12
rivers, 6, 8
roads, 14, 16

San Andreas fault, 21
seasons, 4
settlers, 10, 12
sheep, 12
Siberia, 4
solar panels, 20

tools, 4, 10
trading posts, 14
trenches, 8

vacationers, 18

water, 4, 6, 8
weather, 5
wind turbines, 20